Messages From

A Still Small Voice

Printed by CreateSpace, An Amazon.com Company

Copyright © 2015 by Debi Joy Beakley

All rights reserved

Scripture taken from the New King James Version

Copyright © 1982 by Thomas Nelson, Inc.

Used by permission. All rights reserved.

Dedicated to Jon

You had me promise to write. Here is my first attempt. So Jon, even though you will never have a chance to read the story: this book is for you. I kept my promise.

A Note to the Wonderful Members of Sam's Club in Vero Beach, Florida:

Thank you for your prayers offered on my behalf. As many of you know, I had planned an extensive trip to capture nature pictures for this book. Health situations canceled the trip. God was at my side and not only did this book get written but a growing experience happened during my seclusion and I was able to put together a book titled **Book of Bookmarks: Words of Faith.**

Then I started taking pictures from out my window photographing the only nature I could see. **Out My Window: Life Within the Tree** was born expected to be released in the Fall of 2015. For all of those who were offering heartfelt, across-the-country help for my trip: I hope the disappointment of not attaining the originally planned book will be lessened by the three I was able to produce.

Acknowledgment

Thank you all and may God greatly bless you for your cherished acts of kindness.

Sue Marshall, my deepest gratitude, my dear friend without your late-night phone calls, walking through countless hours of long-distance editing, and your continual encouragement there would be no books.

Brandy Kramer, I am so thankful you had completed your book prior to mine. Instead of laughing at the error of my ways you not only laughed with me but walked me through the final steps from written word to printed publication. You picked me up when I was ready to throw in the towel and taught me a valuable lesson: format last ☺

Charles Harduby, as you could see I truly had a fantastic way to use your deeply appreciated gift of your Mt. Shasta picture on such a beautiful day. Forever grateful.

Table of Contents

God's Peace — 11
God's Peaceful Storm — 13
God's Gift — 15
I Know God Talks to Me — 17

Mountain Drive — 19
Jon's Poem — 21
A Sample of Heaven — 23
Peace on the Mountaintop — 25
Renewal — 27
Rest Easy My Child — 29
Life's Journey — 31
I Wonder — 33
Shadows — 36
The Day's End — 38
The Path — 41
Evening Approaching — 44
A New Day — 46

God's Creations — 47
The Drought — 50
Unseen Beauty — 52
God's Praises — 54
No Man's Hand — 57
The Greatest Gift — 59
I Think of God — 61

Crying Out to God — 63
Help Lord — 65
God Hear My Cry — 68
God Never Leaves — 70
Unconditional Love — 74
God Forgives — 77

God's My Dad   80

God's Answers   *81*
I Am With You Always   84
Why I'm Thankful   86
Help Me Be a Servant   89
A Prayer for a Stranger   91
The Seed   93
Reassurance   96

Parents and Children   *97*
Leaving the Nest   99
A Mother's Love   102
Understanding Father   104
My Mom   106
Playing in the Snow   108

Thoughts At About the Future   *109*
Going Home   111
No Second Chances Needed   113
Commitment   115

Introduction

Have you ever found yourself in a situation you had no control over or that was no fault of your own? Kind of like a wrong place wrong time? Let me share with you that there is no reason to feel alone. Believe me I have been there.

Most of the following pages are filled with what I learned during trying times. Not in a preachy sort of way but more in an eye opening, spirit refreshing, point pondering, private healing experience. At different times throughout my life, usually when everything is turned upside down and inside out I hear a still small voice. I call it a small voice because the sound is almost like a gentle, soft whisper in my spirit. How many times that voice was ignored I will never know, but once I learned to acknowledge it and write down what I was hearing I was surprised at what I read on the paper. For a long time, years, there was never a thought to share any of these poems.

Then one day on my way to work I heard the voice tell me to take the poem that was on my desk to share. Because I worked in a public place I was a little uneasy but could not shake the feeling that it was important. Knowing the result of writing when this voice spoke to me, I said a prayer and followed the feeling. That day was busy at work. I had almost forgotten the morning's events when a regular member came up and asked for the joke of the weekend which in summer was my usual weekend treat.

Working in a seasonal store I had started sharing a "joke of the weekend" to break things up.

Now I was on the spot. I had brought the poem instead of a joke: it was time for my faith to be tested. Explaining what had taken place that morning I asked...really in a sort of, "I only have this poem today and I'm not sure if you would enjoy it but you are welcome to read it if you like." You can tell how, not-so-bold in the faith I was...but I had offered the poem in obedience, so my conscience was clear.

Here came the first surprise: the person not only liked the poem but wanted to know where I had found it, so I explained about the still small voice. I was asked if there were more to share and if so would I bring them. I kept bringing poems to share and people kept asking for copies. During the next few years I learned to share my faith while sharing the poems. The readers of the poems one by one planted the seed of putting this book together. The foundation of this book was being laid but it took a while for me to figure that part out.

When people shared their responses to the poems they used words like comforted, encouraged and inspired. At times there were tears, at other times laughter; mostly they expressed the desire to share what they had read with others.

Now that you find yourself with this book in hand, I pray the words bring you your own personal message from the still small voice. May they speak to your heart and soul. May you be comforted, encouraged and inspired.

Now come let me share with you some life experiences and messages from the still small voice.

God's   Peace

Through the Storms

"Then He arose and rebuked the wind, and said to the sea, 'Peace be still!' And the wind ceased and there was great calm." (Mark 4:39)

I found myself in beautiful Tennessee. The mornings were cool and if you went out onto the porch you could watch the deer coming across the road. The place is a peaceful slice of heaven on earth. As I was busy making a hand stitched quilt, time was passing quickly.

This was my time to be alone to sort out the storms of life: husband Jon's death, son Jason's post-military experiences, lost employment, and the new life I was expected to begin. My favorite sorting place became the front porch all snuggled up and enjoying the surroundings. I was quietly praying that peace would return, asking why, expressing self-pity, and basically explaining to the Lord all about my trials and troubles, complaining about the storms in my life, and how I had to take care of myself. I'm sure you've never done that but I'm still growing so yes, I was complaining. As I am complaining...

The scripture: *"For I, the Lord your God, will hold your right hand, saying to you, fear not, I will help you." (Isaiah 41:13)* came to mind. Being me, I said ok God, then help NOW! Here came the storm....

God's Peaceful Storm (2007)

Out on the porch, wrapped in my blanket warm
I stop to enjoy God's peaceful storm
He watches through the lightning; His touch is in the rain
But it is in the thunder when I hear Him call my name

The lightning is flashing across the sky
Bringing the outline of trees to my watchful eye
The sky sometimes opens from the piercing light
Splitting open the sky on God's stormy night

Drizzle has started to dampen the ground
Raindrops are falling without making a sound
They fall so softly, a gentle touch from above
For God is now showing nature His love

The roar of the thunder is distant and then
A close crash of thunder tells me it's Him
Talking to me through this peaceful storm
Assuring His power against all harm

Without this storm God sent today
I might have faltered and lost my way
But I know this storm was sent for me
'Cause God uses nature when He wants me to see

It's amazing and awesome how far God will go
When He has a message He wants me to know
The message to me this stormy night:

God's storms can bring peace to the storms in my life

The storms of life are no respecter of persons we all at some time share the experience. Have you ever had times in your life when it seemed like no matter how hard you tried nothing made sense? People told me for years, "Put it in God's hands". Well I thought I was doing that: I prayed; made God aware of the situation, forgetting that He is omniscient. I offered my useless suggestions on how God should proceed. This should have you laughing by now. Please God fix this and oh, by the way, this is how I think it would work best. I'm happy you never made such a foolish move.

Well here is the funny part, the more and faster my thoughts and solutions spun around in my mind the harder it was to sleep; strange how that works. I don't understand, what is the matter with me? Back to God: "Lord I'm your child; I just do not understand why you don't fix this. I can't even sleep." God: "Show me you trust me. Go lie down and sleep." With doubt- filled hesitation I opened the window and heading for bed opened the Bible to read, *"I will both lie down in peace, and sleep. For You alone, O Lord, make me dwell in safety."* (Psalm 4:8). I started to gaze out the window meditating on what I had just read….

God's Gift (2007)

The stars they shown so brightly
In the stillness of the night
With each twinkle they sent out
A bright and glorious light

I knew that I could touch them
If I reached into the sky
They seemed so close beside me
My mind it wondered why
God would send His silent gift
To such... a one... as I

I asked why He gave this present
Of a beautiful starlit sky
I heard His voice so softly
Whispering, "Child you are mine.
I sent the stars to show you
I'll watch over you through the night."

When I lay down to sleep
A peace came over me
As through my bedroom window
God's gift I still could see

Do you notice the voices of life? Well-meaning people who only have your best interest at heart just keep talking, offering helpful advice. Children need your attention to have you really listen to them. Spouses need your input on important decisions. Employers want to share their latest greatest company ideas. A co-worker wants to know your secret of success. Everywhere you turn voices fill your thoughts and your emotions.

When life has me to the point of my own thoughts shouting to be heard: that is the time I head for nature. It is time to rejuvenate myself with stillness, peace and immediate quiet. After a few moments surrounded by nature I can begin to hear the sounds of God's creation; along with that comes God's own voice.

God says, *"My sheep hear My voice, and I know them, and they follow Me." (John 10:27).* After my nature timeout with God I am a much better listener. His voice fills my soul with peace, my spirit with harmony, and my heart with love for others.

I Know God Talks to Me (2007)

As the breeze whispers
Through the leaves of the trees
I can hear God talking to me

As the crickets are chirping
And the bullfrogs they sing
I can hear God talking to me

When the thunder roars
And the gurgling brook flows by
I can hear God talking to me

No human voice do I hear
Only nature's sounds fall on my ear

But my heart, it knows

<u>GOD</u>

Is talking to me

Mountain Drive

A Journey of Strength

"And He said to me, 'My grace is sufficient for you, for My strength is made perfect in weakness.' Therefore most gladly I would rather boast in my infirmities, that the power of Christ may rest upon me."
(2 Corinthians 12:9)

One of Jon's favorite places was Blue Lake in northern California, an interesting mountain drive full of beauty. Being from New Jersey, northern California was a new world for him. One of Jon's requests was to have some of his ashes scattered on Jess Valley Road, the first place where he had watched eagles soaring through the air and their nest was so close he said he felt he could touch it. Here I was honoring his wish; guess you could say this was a difficult time.

If you have ever experienced having a loved one pass you know there are no words. Many major life events could compare with a death. You learn quickly life does not stop. The pain feels as if it will never diminish. People console you. You want *them* to feel better but you're devoid of emotions except pain. God is someone you question. Faith, how do you function; Faith, how do you trust; Faith, will the pain stop? Hold on to God, let Him comfort you, give up asking why. I'm still learning to *"Trust in the Lord with all your heart, and lean not on your own understanding; in all your ways acknowledge Him, and He shall direct your paths."* (Proverbs 3:5-6).

The next series of poems were written coming down that mountain.

Jon's Poem (2011)

By the babbling brook
Where the eagles fly
As the mountaintops
Reach up to touch the sky

I took my loved one
To say goodbye
For now with Jesus
He does reside

I miss him more
Each day he's gone
But I have faith
It won't be long

When we'll be together
Again you see
Forever with Jesus
Through eternity

I'd like to be
With him so free
Right now God says
It's not time for me

God kept me here
So I'll do my best
To show God's love
To all the rest...
                Of His children

Needing fresh air I got out of the car and found a fallen tree. Sitting down I noticed a splash of color in the air. This time of day everything was silent. As I settled down I began to notice colors in the air. Suddenly I realized I was watching a field of butterflies. A layer over the field was alive with radiant colors floating silent and free.

Probably because of my mission, the jewel tones in the air before me made me think of the beauty I remember reading about that is awaiting us in heaven. *"The construction of its wall was of jasper; and the city was pure gold, like clear glass. The foundations of the wall of the city were adorned with all kinds of precious stones:...jasper... sapphire...chalcedony...emerald... sardonyx...sardius...chrysolite...beryl...topaz...chrysoprase... jacinth...amethyst. The twelve gates were twelve pearls...the street was pure gold..."* (Revelation 21:18-21).

I thanked God for sharing His field of beauty that no man could create. Giving me true peace through unexpected beauty was helping my spirit heal.

A Sample of Heaven (2011)

I watched the butterflies

Floating by

Peaceful and calm

Against the sky

Their beauty was beyond compare

As visions of colors

Sailed through the air

God shares them with others

So we can see

A sample of heaven

Spirits so free

With visions of jewels floating through the air it was time to start moving. Just a little way down the road was the eagle's nest. Finding a place to pull off the road I stepped back in time for just a moment. Laughter, tears and peace all in the blink of an eye flooded my emotions. The still small voice: *"Peace I leave with you, My peace I give to you; not as the world gives do I give to you. Let not your heart be troubled, neither let it be afraid."(John 14:27).*

Ok God, I'll try not to be troubled. I could have just stayed there till the end of time. Let life stop. Of course we have no choice in the matter: life will continue. So, back in the car; only problem: I still felt troubled. "Well God, any idea when this peace is coming?" I heard Pastor Jentezen Franklin mention in His sermon Made for More: A Place Called Yonder: "We are a microwave generation but serve a crock-pot God".

Not sure about you; maybe patience comes naturally, or it is your gift. Unfortunately, I am not known for waiting well. I just want to complete the mission. God's timing is perfect. I know this… but…you know… growing in our walk with God is not easy…

Peace on the Mountaintop (2011)

Clouds above the mountaintop floating by

Make me wish I were an eagle so I could fly

Sailing through the air my spirit so free

Reaching out to God and Eternity

The peace they bring my soul today

I know is from God in His own way

I noticed the eagle coming back to its nest as I started pulling onto the road. He looked peaceful sailing on the currents. For a second I felt a twinge of peace. Then the thoughts started spinning as I was driving. So I talked to God, "I am not going to be able to function much longer. I am overwhelmed here God. I can't do this I need you to fix this NOW!" You have to love God's sense of humor. I calmed down and was praying...then the still small voice.

God's reply: *"But those who **wait** on the Lord, shall renew their strength; they shall mount up with wings like eagles, they shall run and not be weary, they shall walk and not faint." (Isaiah 40:31)*. Ok God, I get it... you are not going to repair my entire life while I drive down this mountain, but you will give me strength during the wait.

Do you ever have a period of feeling overwhelmed? Feel as if you are being pulled in fifty different directions and no one around can see you need help? Trust this: God does see and He will help. The only catch: in His own time. What do we do? Pray, help others and wait on the Lord.

Renewal *(2011)*

Mountains so rugged
Solid and strong

Nourish my soul
When life feels so wrong

The earth it seems to
Talk to me

While walking in nature
Peaceful and free

There is no place
I would rather be

Than living in nature
God's gift to me

Let go and let God take care of things. Ever had a person tell you that? Well I had lots of well-meaning people telling me. Sometimes I wanted to scream: "My problem is not a balloon that I can take outside and let the string go and all will be well." I needed strength, rest, peace and the problem was I was trying to find those things on my own.

At this point I was beginning to see only God could provide the strength, rest, and peace I so desperately needed. I had even tried to bury myself in church work. Maybe if I volunteered enough God would what...at that point I almost thought I needed to buy God's help. Funny how far off track our spinning minds can take us. Well my mind had stopped spinning and I was in a place where I could once again hear the still small voice.

So I prayed, "God please help. I can't go back home and face life alone." It was then I heard: *"Come to Me, all you who labor and are heavy laden, and I will give you rest. Take My yoke upon you and learn from Me, for I am gentle and lowly in heart, and you will find rest for your souls."* (Matthew 11:28-29).

Lesson here when your mind is spinning: turn to the Word. Saves a lot of time.

Rest Easy My Child (2011)

Trees on the mountaintops
Standing silent and strong
Giving me strength
While singing a song

With the help of the wind
Passing through the leaves
A message from God
They are bringing to me

Rest easy my child
I hear them say
God will give you strength
To face another day

Just plant your roots
On solid ground
Never forget
God is always around

To soothe your soul
And bring you peace
When all of your pain
To Him you release

I had reached a place on the road where it is fun when you go down; then you go up till you can't see the road ahead. How like my life at that moment. One side has a river, the other side has a cliff. I was really watching the white line.

Knowing I would be headed back to Florida in a few days, the churning of emotions had already begun. I decided to pull over. That part of the road always made me a little nervous and I already had white knuckles.

Getting out of the car, this time I took a different approach. Sometimes in mountain areas sound will echo; this was one of those places. I began to sing praises. As my own peace offering to the Lord. Heading back to the car I felt a little different, calmer, a little more at peace. Just in case God was not aware, I thought I might remind Him that life in Florida felt like the sight I was staring at: wide open spaces full of vast emptiness and void of any direction. The voice reminded me I did have a map for life. *"Your word is a lamp to my feet and a light to my path."* (Psalm 119:105).

I was learning this lesson: don't spin, turn to His Word, our roadmap for life.

Life's Journey (2011)

The ups and downs of a mountain road

Are like watching the years of my life unfold

The line in the middle keeps guiding me

To my home someday in Eternity

God's word is my roadmap, His gift to me

Guiding me daily, keeping me free

Leading the way through the darkest night

Always reassuring everything is all right

The Bible, the Word of God, is our life's roadmap. I will admit I was not spending enough time in the Word. Years of praying for Jon's salvation, then he accepted Jesus, an excited baby Christian, and BAM within TEN MONTHS he was gone. There were people who told me God took him home so he did not have time to fall back in his old ways!?! I was there as he tried to figure out how to help others "meet God" as soon as he was healed. The comments weighed heavily on my mind. Have you ever had people trying to help actually destroy you and never even know what they did?

I was very depressed actually for almost nine years, barely functioning except in public and never leaving the house unless necessary. "Well God...I know Jon was saved I was there. But he was a baby in you...is he with you? He was sick unto death with no time to grow in you..."thoughts spinning: "God help".

This drive was enabling me to grow in leaps and bounds. So I asked God and heard, *"Assuredly, I say to you, whoever does not receive the kingdom of God as a little child will by no means enter it." (Mark 10:15-16).*

I Wonder (2011)

I wonder if heaven has mountains

I wonder what kind they will be

I wonder if heaven has nature

I wonder if God made it for me

As a child did you ever lie on your back on the lawn and look up at the clouds? We did, trying to see what pictures we could find. Wonder: what an interesting word. One definition is a feeling of amazement, puzzled interest, or reverent admiration. Looking at the mountains with the sun starting to lower in the sky, it seemed like, as for Joshua, the sun was almost standing still for me. *"Then Joshua spoke to the Lord.... So the sun stood still, and the moon stopped."* (Joshua 10:12-13).

It seemed God was slowing the sun to give me time on the mountain to heal. Each stop as He spoke to me I felt strength building. I had stopped to watch the shadows create transforming designs on the side of the rock wall. My mind was relaxing in God's peace. There was the eagle sailing high above the riverbed. His shadow crossed over the windshield and I thought, *"Because You have been my help, therefore in the shadow of Your wings I will rejoice. My soul follows close behind You; Your right hand upholds me."* (Psalm 63:7-8).

Strength was building, faith was returning, and peace was saturating my broken spirit. Finally, I was coming to a place where I knew my job was to trust God and rest in His peace. The peaceful scene in front of me, a sight God created, was my example of peace. I could live in His peace.

Then the slight doubt: how do I know for certain? This time I had my own answer, *"God is not a man, that He should lie..."* (Numbers 23:19).

If you ever have doubts turn to the Word; you **will** find the answers. I carry a verse to share... a scripture a day helps keep the devil away. This also helps me memorize a verse at a time to hide in my heart.

Shadows (2011)

Shadows falling from mountains

Shadows in shape of the trees

Shadows bringing me visions

Of what the future may be

Evening brings shadows and nightfall

Nightfall brings rest from the day

Rest brings sleep to the weary

Sleep brings dreams far away

Dreams bring me reassurance

Letting me hear what God has to say.

Jon was home in heaven but I still had things to do here on earth. God was showing me I needed to change my focus. I needed to stop being so busy trying to earn approval from others. Instead I should focus on what really mattered: God's love, mercy, and grace. I needed the focus of Jesus' friend Mary: Lazarus and Martha's sister. I was too busy being Martha.

"But Martha was distracted with much serving, and she approached Him and said, 'Lord, do You not care that my sister has left me to serve alone? Therefore tell her to help me.' And Jesus answered and said to her, 'Martha, Martha, you are worried and troubled about many things. But one thing is needed, and Mary has chosen that good part, which will not be taken away from her.'" (Luke 10:40-42).

Choose the good part: Jesus, His love, teachings and sacrifice; that should be my focus. "God you want *me* to *focus*?" For a second I forgot God will not ask me to do anything that He is not by my side. If I stay by Jesus' side I'm safe. If things are spinning for you check where you are focusing: on the good part (Jesus) or on the problem.

The Day's End (2011)

Cool breeze of the evening

Replaces the heat of the day

God's plan of creation

His cycle of life some may say

The cycle of life is very much a reality for me. On the day Jon was diagnosed, literally during the doctor's appointment, the phone rang. There was our son, Jason, informing us our first grandchild was coming *now*: they were at the hospital. There was no time to think. The cycle of life: babies born and 46-year-olds dying.

"Fear not, for I am with you." (Isaiah 43:5).

When bombs drop in your life, remember you are not alone; for every life there is a story. Instead realize we are still here and able to share our stories. You *will* survive. For the first time in years my thoughts were calming down. Reality was setting in; I would be going home alone, yet at the same time God was with me. Funny how you know this, yet fail to remember; an old habit will die hard. There I was, starting to spin. The what ifs, the how's it goings, the I can'ts. I started to hear the small voice but the fear was churning louder than the voice. Then CRACK, I turned around to see a tree falling across the narrow part of the river. That got my attention.

I heard the small voice; I was going to be alright; God had a plan for me. *"Before I formed you in the womb I knew you; before you were born I sanctified you..." (Jeremiah 1:5).* The voice, "You need to trust me completely. I have a plan for you. I will guide you down the path." Ok, well thanks Lord, can't say I really understood. So I asked, "What plan, what path?" Remember patience is not my strong suit.

I looked back to where the tree had fallen. Then like a bolt I got it: the tree over the river was like the path God had for me. I can only see part at a time. Ouch! I want the whole map not just the starting path.

The Path (2011)

Rugged cliffs and glistening peaks

Dotted by the trees

Fallen branches across the brook

Making a path for me

A path? Well we don't always get what we want. But I had GOD. I'm not sure if you like life a little at a time or if you are a complete picture person. I am a complete picture person to a fault. You could ask my family; on second thought *please* don't. There was comfort realizing God would not leave me. There was regret that I had forgotten God; never beneficial to put God on a back burner of your life.

God was bringing me safely down the mountain with His perfect timing. The sun was only a slight distance from dropping behind the mountaintops.

At that moment the peace was so palpable the car felt like being enclosed in a pressure cooker. I was smothered with peace inside and out. Stillness like I had never known. I just wanted to stop the car and stay forever. My mind started to race with fear. Would I ever feel this kind of peace again? I was afraid to move for fear the peace would leave. Sounds a little out there, I know. If you have never experienced the flood of peace, I really can't explain it but I pray you share the experience someday. If you have experienced the flood of peace then you know exactly what I mean.

Now I was strong. Not becoming strong. I was/am strong. It was time to head to the bottom of the mountain. While I was driving I felt as if God asked me if I was willing to pick up my cross and follow Him down the path He has for me. The scripture came to mind: *"Then He said to them all, 'If anyone desires to come after Me, let him deny himself, and take up his cross daily, and follow Me. For whoever desires to save his life will lose it, but whoever loses his life for My sake will save it. For what profit is it to a man if he gains the whole world, and is himself destroyed or lost? For whoever is ashamed of Me and My words, of him the Son of Man will be ashamed when He comes in His own glory, and in His Father's, and of the holy angels.'" (Luke 9:23-26).* Wow, was I ready? To be honest, right then I'm not sure I was but in faith I said yes.

This time of day the mountain seemed calm. I felt like I should stop once more. All this time I had been writing the poems on any paper I could find in the rental car. I had left on a mission to fulfill a promise. Instead I found myself on a personal journey of strength with God as my personal tour guide. The sunset had begun…

Evening Approaching *(2011)*

Sunset it is coming soon

Rest within the woods

Stillness of the nighttime falls

Ending the day as only God could

End of day, time to face reality. What a wonderful God timeout. I had kept my promise to Jon. I knew I was healing, growing, and learning to trust. I was finding my way back to God, my Dad.

I had begged God to take me and leave Jon. That was not God's plan. For a while I was angry at God. An absolutely ridiculous reaction but we can't change facts. I had been trying through it all to find my way back but had been too full of self-pity and unwarranted anger to make any sense. Now my mind was clear.

God had a plan for me? What could *I* do? If you ever ask yourself these questions know, *"But God has chosen the foolish things of the world to put to shame the wise, and God has chosen the weak things of the world to put to shame the things which are mighty." (1 Corinthians 1:27)*. I had no idea the scraps of paper (the poems) sitting on the dashboard would, just a few years later, be in the hands of strangers. I had no idea, but **God** did. There was one more stop at the bottom of the mountain. Such a precious scene was unfolding in the middle of the forest. As I was drinking in the sight before me I heard the small voice, *"...that you may walk worthy of the Lord, fully pleasing Him, being fruitful in every good work and increasing in the knowledge of God; strengthened with all might, according to His glorious power, for all patience and longsuffering with joy; giving thanks to the Father who has qualified us to be partakers of the inheritance of the saints in the light". (Colossians 1:10-12)*. The strength and joy I was feeling was from the Lord. God has a plan for me. And you know God has a plan for your life also.

A New Day (2011)

Deer drinking beside the brook

The fawns they are so small

Trees are standing close beside

Silent and so strong

Makes a person stop and think

Of life in every way

God's abounding gift of creation

Ever-changing each new day

I hope you were strengthened during our Mountain drive. God does not have any favorites what he did for me He will do for you. Just ask Him.

God's Creations

Nature at its finest

"In the beginning God created the heavens and the earth." (Genesis 1:1).

During my time in Tennessee the area was experiencing the worst drought in many decades. The first rain to fall was the night the skies opened up and the small voice gave me the words to "God's Peaceful Storm". That evening I had been watching the weather and the interviews with local townsfolk praying for rain. There was no indication that rain was expected anytime soon.

I think it caught my attention as much as it did because of the drought I had been living. Have you ever had a personal drought? A place where everything seems to dry up and stop, be it finances, relationships, or your own personal ambition.

The Bible shares a situation concerning Elijah and a devastating drought. Ahab, King of Israel, had led the people to worship Baal. God sent Elijah with a message. *"And Elijah...said to Ahab, 'As the Lord God of Israel lives, before whom I stand, there shall not be dew nor rain these years, except at my word.'" (1 Kings 17:1).* The people in Elijah's time lived through three years of drought, but God had not forgotten them. There was a problem though: they kept wavering between God and Baal. It was time to make a choice. Sometimes in life God seems far away, although He never is, but our actions can cause a spiritual drought. There are choices that we need to make. Find what is robbing our time with God or the things that cause God to slide down our list of priorities, and make the changes.

Elijah knew that worshiping Baal was the problem; the people needed to choose. God also used Elijah to prove no matter how the odds against you appear, with God on your side you will prevail. Elijah was God's prophet; there were 450 prophets worshiping Baal. Those are some drastic odds: one against 450. God had Elijah host a contest of sorts; you can find the details in 1Kings 18. Final outcome: God won. Then Elijah prayed, in faith believing, and started sending his servant to check for rain. *"Then it came to pass the seventh time, that he said, 'There is a cloud, as small as a man's hand, rising out of the sea!' ... the sky became black with clouds and wind, and there was a heavy rain."(1Kings 18:44-45).* God lets us learn but He never leaves us.

The Drought *(2007)*

No stars shine
No moon glows
The night sky darkens
God creates His storm

Wind whips
Thunder rolls
Lightning flashes
God sends His storm

Raindrops fall
Rivers flood
Mankind awakens
God sent His storm

Cornfields drink
Gardens flourish
Earth replenished
God provides with His storm

Concerns removed
Fear subsides
Worries vanish
God teaches through His storm

Farmers praise
Children sleep
Men rejoice
God blesses by His storm

Storms or droughts, either way God always has our best interest at heart. We can turn to Him through anything. A great scripture to remember is, *"For He commanded and they were created." (Psalm 148:5).* In Genesis we read about God's creation. He spoke; it became: that's POWER. When we know God, and His power, how can we allow life's obstacles to overtake our worlds?

When fear starts I remind myself that God takes care of all His creations including you and me. He is faithful. You see it 24 hours a day if you just take your eyes off your circumstances and observe His handiwork. Enjoy what we can see and realize how much we will never see. *"Praise the Lord from the earth…snow and clouds, stormy wind…mountains and all hills…" (Psalm 148:7-9).*

Unseen Beauty (2007)

Did you ever want to see

Untouched nature so pristine

Meant for us to wonder so

Unreachable places we'll never know

Mountains and trees: I love their appearance, much like humans, similar yet with their own individuality. God, it seems, does not create any two things alike. Do you see the way trees point to the sky? Sometimes I wonder when the breeze is blowing through the branches if that is their praise offering.

I notice in the mornings before the birds search for food there is the sound of singing and chirping. For years I have believed they are talking to our creator. Maybe we should take a tip from nature and acknowledge God first in our day rather than as our 'on call' God. There is a plan for our lives but if we make different choices God will find someone to perform the task.

Jesus made this clear to the Pharisees, who wanted Him to rebuke His disciples for praising Him as they entered Jerusalem. *"But He answered and said to them, 'I tell you that if these should be silent, the stones would immediately cry out.'" (Luke 19:40).*

God gives so much and requests so little. I hope His beautiful unmatchable nature will nourish your spirit and soul, drawing you closer to a more intimate relationship with our Creator. And unlike the world, His gifts are free: the price has already been paid in full.

God's Praises (2007)

Mountain peaks so high

Reaching up towards the sky

Topped with trees so ever green

Filled with birds: God's praises sing

From Genesis to Revelation we are reminded God created all things. *"You are worthy oh Lord, to receive glory and honor and power. For You created all things and by Your will they exist and were created". (Revelation 4:11)*. I think that means creation is something worthy of our attention and gratitude.

"Thus says God the Lord, Who created the heavens and stretched them out, Who spread forth the earth and that which comes from it, who gives breath to the people on it...I, the Lord, have called you in righteousness, and will hold your hand..." (Isaiah 42:5-6). Our every breath comes from God and He holds our hand. What more could we ask of Him?

Yet, life takes over and God, 'giver of our every breath' takes a back seat because we have to handle life. In the moment that thought process makes perfect sense but looking at the big picture, especially if you factor in eternity, let's just say it may not make as much sense.

Oh, I have an idea what you are thinking...the bill is in my name; I was at work when the school called me; the schedule to be met is mine. See, I get it: 'my, me, mine' and let's not forget 'I'. In the world's eyes you are 100 percent correct. Problem is from God's point of view: why are we worried?

He gave us life, He holds our hand, He never forsakes us, and His proof you can check right now...are you breathing? I know I am; yes, I experience stress and all the negative emotions the world has to offer but I desperately try to remind myself *I am breathing* therefore God is in control.

Since God is in control why not try to relax with nature; that's my secret: I can find it almost anywhere, it's a gift I could never purchase, and God made it to be enjoyed.

No Man's Hand (2007)

Wildlife in the woods so deep

Keep the secrets we still seek

Of the beauty deep within

Created by God and not by men

Watching children playing outdoors is pure delight; they understand nature. Lost in world of dirt, sand, grass, rocks, flowers and trees they can stay occupied for hours. They find bugs, lizards, butterflies and frogs. Things that amaze them we hardly even notice. Take them to the beach and unless they are exhausted, getting them to leave is a job in itself. All they seem to realize is nature is a world of fantastic life.

Guess you could say they are in agreement with the great creator God Himself. The Bible says: *"So God created great sea creatures and every living thing that moves, with which the waters abounded, according to their kind, and every winged bird according to its kind. And God saw that it was good"*. *(Genesis 1:21).*

The Greatest Gift *(2007)*

Walking by the lake so blue

I had to stop and think of you

Creator of everything large and small

What is your greatest gift of all?

Could it be mountains, lakes and skies

Or oceans deep where many secrets lie?

That is what I did believe

Until your salvation I received

Salvation is the greatest gift by far. Yet, God in His infinite compassion wanted us to enjoy life on earth as well. I think nature was one of His ways to help us. God knew our time on earth would have heartache and turmoil so He gave us His Word to guide us down the narrow path. His Word is filled with compassion, instruction, and intervention. Life is hectic to say the least. I listened to Joyce Meyer's teaching, "Where the Mind Goes, the Man Follows," so many times I have portions almost memorized. The lessons hit home with me: what have I been thinking? Where did I let my mind focus? Was I thinking on the goodness of God and how no situation is too difficult for Him to handle? Or was I thinking about the problems? Can you guess? You're correct: problems. I became proactive.

I started taking a scripture a day from my promise box and putting it in my pocket. I read it when I felt stressed, I read it throughout the day, and I used it to help others feeling tension. Some days I thought the verse might wear out before day's end, but two things: one, that never happened and two, the verse always turned out to fit the situation perfectly. You might want to try this trick: it helps you keep living the verse, *"Finally, brethren, whatever things are true, whatever thing are noble, whatever things are just, whatever things are pure, whatever things are lovely, whatever things are of good report, if there is any virtue and if there is anything praise-worthy-meditate on these things" (Philippians 4:8).*

I Think of God (2007)

As I'm watching the sparrows
Feeding their young
I think of God

When I spot the shy fawn
Run through the open pond
I think of God

I think of God
Whose Son shone brightly
In a world that was lost and unsightly
And my dream you see
To be…much more like Him
Much less like me
And so
I think of God

Secure and on my way
To a bright and better day
I think of God

Then someday I will know
As I view His glorious glow

God

He thought of me

Crying Out to God

When life gives you lemons

"Hear my cry, O God; Attend to my prayer."
(Psalm 61:1)

Was there ever a time when you thought "God do you see me? Do you hear me? How do you expect me to handle this...?" When You know God does hear, see, and have a plan but all you *feel* is empty and lost? You're in good company. David cried out to God; *"Hear, O Lord, when I cry with my voice! Have mercy also upon me, and answer me. When You said, 'Seek My face,' my heart said to You, 'Your face, Lord, I will seek.' Do not hide Your face from me; do not turn Your servant away in anger; You have been my help; do not leave nor forsake me, O God of my salvation." (Psalm 27:7-9).*

David was a *"man after God's own heart."* Most of the 150 Psalms were penned by David; they are a combination of tears, anguish and rejoicing. David passed his love and knowledge of God to his son.

"And David said to his son Solomon, 'Be strong and of good courage, and do it; do not fear nor be dismayed, for the Lord God-my God- will be with you. He will not leave you nor forsake you, until you have finished all the work for the service of the house of the Lord.'" (1Chronicles 28:20).

Help Lord

God where are you?

I feel so lost

I forgot to put you first

Am I now paying the cost?

Everything seems far away

And getting farther everyday

I'm so weary I just can't move

Lord won't you tell me what to do?

You know what's best for me right now

Won't you show me some way, somehow?

I'm only happy serving you

Lord please tell me what to do

Solomon had his earthly dad, David, and Joshua had his mentor, Moses. *"Then Moses called Joshua and said to him in the sight of all Israel, 'Be strong and of good courage...And the Lord...will be with you; He will not leave you nor forsake you, do not fear nor be dismayed.'"* (Deuteronomy 31:7-8).

Who do you have to encourage you? Yes, we have God to guide and direct us. Did you know He puts people in our lives to encourage us, reprimand us with love, and lend us a shoulder for our tears? Are you that person to someone? Do you let your person know how valuable they are to you? *Hebrews 10:24-25 tells us, "And let us consider one another in order to stir up love and good works, not forsaking the assembling of ourselves together, as is the manner of some, but exhorting one another...".*

Sometime when you are at a gathering, take a moment and ask God to show you a person to encourage. You may just be surprised at who He puts in your path. We are experts at putting on the game face. *I can't let you know I'm hurting, worried, or lonely. What would you think? I'm the go-to person. I'm the one who gets things done. I'm not human.* Sound familiar? How do I know? I was that person. I could have had a Master's Degree. I was known as the encourager, helper, always willing to do the unnoticed. My heart was willing but my soul was empty. How about a man's analogy: my car wanted to go but the gas tank was empty. No one had any idea this was the real me: *"Bow down Your ear, O Lord, hear me; for I am poor and needy. Preserve my life, for I am holy; You are my God; save Your servant who trusts in You! Be merciful to me, O Lord, for I cry to You all day long. Rejoice the soul of Your servant, for to You, O Lord, I lift up my soul. For You, Lord, are good, and ready to forgive, and abundant in mercy to all those who call upon You. Give ear, O Lord, to my prayer; and attend to the voice of my supplications. In the day of my trouble I will call upon You, for You will answer me." (Psalm 86:1-7).*

God Hear My Cry *(2010)*

The days are filled with stress

I cry to God just let me rest

Too many demands are placed on me

I feel I'm drowning in life's sea

Honesty is not easy when pride is involved. Hurting people do not wear name badges. Those two things make a bad combination. If you are hurting ask God to help you find a grounded, seasoned, Christian, a person of your same sex ('Women from Venus, Men from Mars' type thing) that can encourage you. Share your situation; ask for prayer or an accountability partner, whatever will ease your pain.

But on the other hand if you are at a strong point in your life right now, then ask God to show you the person who needs a helping hand. Kingdom work is all that counts in the end. We all have weak times and most of us will be filled with strength at other times. Once in a while we just need a helping hand to jump-start life.

There is a little twist: if you are down, one of the quickest ways to refocus your thinking is to help others. I do not mean go to church Sunday and sign up for everything looking for a volunteer. That might just be part of how you lost focus. Find a simple task to help one person. An elderly lady on the block who would love a hello as you walk the dog, maybe take her a flower from your yard. If you see a student standing in the rain at the bus stop have the child sit in the car with yours. A simple task; the Bible says in *Zechariah 4:10, "For who has despised the day of small things?"* I think God watches to see if we notice the simple needs He places in our path each day. *"I will bring the blind by a way they did not know; I will lead them in paths they have not known. I will make darkness light before them, and crooked places straight. These things I will do for them, and not forsake them." (Isaiah 42:16).*

God Never Leaves (2014)

Though the tears are coming

The birds sing from the trees

The pain is so heartbreaking

You're not alone I hear them sing

God He is with you

God will guide you to either find help or be the helper. Always remember regardless of the problems, *"For He Himself has said, 'I will never leave you nor forsake you.' So we may boldly say: 'The Lord is my helper; I will not fear. What can man do to me?'" (Hebrews 13:5-6)*. If your problem is a people problem memorize the verse above. Here is an important point to remember: God is greater than any human situation.

I experienced a true human situation recently. I had been praying for a few years about relocating. The city I lived in had grown to the point where seeing the stars at my house was a thing of the past. Sometimes we should remember all that glitters is not gold. I found this lovely place with mature Live Oaks on an acre where the stars light up the sky on a clear night. Peaceful and quiet except for the sounds of nature. Looked and sounded just like my prayer. So I relocated. Then came the human situation. Ever have a friend for years, a person you trusted, a person who cared? Then find out the ugly side of life. Welcome to my world.

Suddenly and violently I found myself in a strange new area where I was completely alone and, I will admit, scared. I had bought the place, so packing and leaving was not an option. I had been working on the books but now my focus was shattered. I did not seem to be able to hear God. I prayed, studied, listened to great teachers and preachers; still nothing. Then I heard ONE word: *Forgive*. What? God, really? You must be kidding. Did you see what happened? God, do You realize that I did nothing wrong? There are witnesses: I did nothing, absolutely nothing wrong. Again I heard *forgive*. I would like to tell you I hit my knees and prayed, got on the phone and forgave the human but… nope don't think so. I'm sorry God, but that is just a little too much to ask. Any reason or excuse I could find I offered up to God. I knew it was *my* life that had been turned upside down and God wants *me* to forgive. God said *nothing*.

Then I remembered: *"But I say to you who hear: Love your enemies, do good to those who hate you, bless those who curse you, and pray for those who spitefully use you. To him who strikes you on the one cheek, offer the other also. And from him, who takes away your cloak, do not withhold your tunic either. Give to everyone who asks of you. And from him who takes away your goods do not ask them back. And just as you want men to do to you, you also do to them likewise…But love your enemies, do good, and lend, hoping for nothing in return; and your reward will be great, and you will be sons of the Most High. For He is kind to the unthankful and evil. Therefore be merciful, just as your Father also is merciful."* (Luke 6: 27-36).

Well it took a while; you should know I am a little stubborn along with being impatient. Eventually, I realized God was not going to give me a single word for the books until I forgave the human. Just about the time I was going to call (I had rehearsed the 'forgive you' call), I heard that still small voice say, "You must mean it from the heart or don't bother." Ouch!

Well that took a couple more days; come on now, Rome was not built in a day either. I know you would have hurried to the phone on the first 'forgive;' if so I admire your level of maturity and hope someday to be there as well. I made the call from the heart and God is giving me words for the books. The roller coaster of life is slowing down. Do you ever feel like you are on the roller coaster? You're locked in no matter the twist and turns. Solution: hold onto God.

Unconditional Love *(2014)*

Who do you trust? How can you tell?

When your mind is spinning

Days and nights seem like hell

God please remind me

Your love it never fails

Did you know roller coasters slow down but that does not mean they are ready to stop? Life can be like that at times; you hit a pocket of cruise control and all appears to be going well and then come the twists and turns. I hope I am not the only one who has had this type of experience. Why would I say that? Because it is holding onto God's hand through the twists and turns that develops our faith. I can't lie and say it is a grand experience but I can tell you that when the roller coaster stops you will find yourself with a deeper personal relationship with God.

It is kind of like 'don't pray for patience' because God will allow situations to come your way so you can learn patience. I don't recommend asking for a roller coaster ride with God. I promise, just wait awhile: there is a car on the track with your name on it. Before your car arrives you may want to ponder this: *"Teach me Your way, O Lord, and lead me in a smooth path, because of my enemies. Do not deliver me to the will of my adversaries; for false witnesses have risen against me, and such as breathe out violence. I would have lost heart, unless I had believed that I would see the goodness of the Lord in the land of the living. Wait on the Lord; be of good courage, and He shall strengthen your heart; wait, I say, on the Lord!" (Psalm 27:11-14).*

Waiting and writing, that is what I was doing and here comes the human. *"Take heed to yourselves. If your brother sins against you, rebuke him; and if he repents, forgive him. And if he sins against you seven times in a day, and seven times in a day returns to you, saying 'I repent', you shall forgive him." (Luke 17:3-4).* I get it God, I know what I am supposed to do but what about the human? This circumstance is getting worse. And I heard, *"You will not need to fight in this battle. Position yourselves, stand still and see the salvation of the Lord, who is with you... 'Do not fear or be dismayed... for the Lord is with you.'"(2 Chronicles 20:17)*. When I heard the scripture I felt His presence. I'm learning more each day: God is with me; He is aware; He is teaching me.

God Forgives (2014)

Friends and family are gone

I realize I'm alone

Wrong choices I have made

Mistakes they are my own

The cry comes from my heart

God please heal the pain

The only thought I'm holding

God's child I remain

Learning is a funny thing. I loved school.

But when life's roller coaster took me for a ride as a teen: I was unable to complete high school. Jump way, way, way ahead and in my very early 40's I took 24 high school classes to earn my diploma. So if you have anything… which you are considering…and think 'it might be too late' know that it is never too late when God is in it with you. God is our father and He only wants to help us and at times maybe even save us from ourselves. So like any dad He has to teach us.

God's school is a different type of classroom. He teaches using real life situations. Have you noticed some life lessons we learn rather easily and for other lessons we go around, and around, and around the mountain? From Exodus to 2015 someone somewhere is always going around the mountain. How can the classroom be so easy and the world so difficult? Well I have learned a few lessons recently, forgiveness for one.

Once God took over the battle, the human became occupied with several situations…thus allowing me peace for now. God keeps His word. *"My covenant I will not break, nor alter the word that has gone out of My lips."* (Psalm 89:34). The Bible is filled with God's promises; isn't it nice to know He keeps His word.

All of God's promises are for all of His children. One promise that is very close to my heart is, *"A father of the fatherless, a defender of widows, is God in His holy habitation."* (Psalm 68:5). A father's love from God almighty... how special we must truly be to Him. I can testify when the world steps out, don't panic: as long as God is with you there is nothing to fear. When you are on life's roller coaster remember He is in the car with you.

God's My Dad (2014)

I belong to no one except God's only son

Sitting on the sidelines, watching others have their fun

My heart is sad and lonely; peace I cannot find

But God is whispering to me:

Child you are mine

God is with us. He is our Father; we can take anything to Him at any time. We seem to be able to take problems to God but have a harder time remembering to thank Him. God gives mercy so I believe God has feelings. I wonder if a thank-you might make God smile. It's just a thought...

God's Answers

In His perfect timing

"But he said to me, 'The Lord, before whom I walk, will send His angel with you and prosper your way...'"
(Genesis 24:40)

God does answer prayers but we need to understand He answers in His timing. *"God is faithful, by whom you were called into the fellowship of His Son, Jesus Christ our Lord." (1Corinthians 1:9).* As you have read over and over throughout this book, God will not leave us nor forsake us. I have shared that thought continually because, at least for me, I know this deep down in my heart but...when trouble arises somehow my thoughts turn to 'how am *I* going to take care of this'. What a difference when we learn to think God *first*.

God is first to a lot of folks on Sunday; we walk out of church knowing God is invincible. But by noon on Monday when life takes over where do our thoughts turn? Do we immediately return to Sunday euphoria and say, "Hi God, I know you see what is happening. I am so thankful you will take care of this for me. And God, since I trust you I am going to leave this problem with you and go about the rest of my day." Sounds great right? I know Christians who have this level of faith: no matter the obstacle they simply give it to God and go about their business. It is not second nature for them it is their FIRST instinct. Question is how many of us live that type of life? We want to, we know we should, yet we falter.

One thing I know for certain: when we go to God first the situations take a lot less time to be resolved, but for some reason we continue to go around the mountain. I think God simply watches and waits for us to mature in our faith. I do believe there is a period of rejoicing in heaven when we finally find our path away from the mountain. Sometimes I am amazed at God's patience. He really wants to spend time with us: time when we come to honor Him, bask in His presence, and every once in a while just stop and spend time with Him like you do with a friend when you are going out to dinner. God has even left us an open invitation, *"Behold, I stand at the door and knock. If anyone hears My voice and opens the door, I will come in to him and dine with him, and he with Me."* (Revelation 3:20).

While we are here on earth we usually won't see God sitting across the table from us. God shows Himself to us in several other ways so we need to learn how God reveals His majesty. Seasoned Christians, this is where you can help babes in Christ. *"'...Teaching them to observe all things that I have commanded you; and lo, I am with you always, even to the end of the age. Amen.'"* (Matthew 28:20).

I Am With You Always *(2013)*

I am listening when you cry out in pain,
"Where are you God? Do you see me down here? Show me a sign. Why
don't you notice me?"

I am with you in the trees
Providing you shade and a place for children to play
But you don't notice me

I am with you in the flowers
Giving you a gift of beautiful colors and sweet fragrance
But you don't notice me

I am in the air
Keeping you alive with every breath
But you don't notice me

I am in the clouds
Silently drifting by, hoping you'll look up and see
But you don't notice me

I am in the rain
Replenishing the oceans, bringing life to the earth
But you don't notice me

I am asking you,
"My child, why don't *you* notice **ME**?"

I am answering your cries continually
In the trees, the flowers, the air, the clouds and the rain
Stop. Be still; take a moment and notice ME.

I am with you always.

Now that is something to be thankful for; seems everywhere we turn God is showing us His presence. Stop. Be still. Take a minute as you walk to your car. Look to the sky and rejoice: God allowed you to have another day. Regardless of what is happening in our lives, we are still here; God kept us through the night while we were unaware of anything around us: we should rejoice. We did not wake up dead...God granted another day.

A couple of years back I was in the hospital and coded out twice. Not a fun time but there is a funny part: I never knew it until the RN explained to me later what had happened, how they saved my life, and how sorry she was...That might sound strange but...I had a DNR they had not seen in my records so God/they saved my life. She was concerned, so I prayed for her and explained I was here by God's timing not ours. We did what the Bible instructs us to do: *"Rejoice always, pray without ceasing, in everything give thanks; for this is the will of God in Christ Jesus for you."* (1Thessalonians 5:16-18). It is easy to be thankful and sing praises when the sun is brightly shining. But in the darkness of life give thanks. God may be enhancing our growth during the darkness.

Why I'm Thankful (2014)

Thank you Lord
For the peace I feel in the midst of the storm

Thank you Lord
For the wisdom to know when to stay silent and still

Thank you Lord
For Your protection from the unseen bullets from the unknown sources in the background of my life

Thank you Lord
For the angels lending a helping hand and creating peace of mind

Thank you Lord
For the strength to remain calm even though my insides are quaking

Thank you Lord
For caring and loving me even though I am not yet where/what I should be

Thank you Lord
For the tears that you dry in the middle of the night that no one else sees

The Bible says, *"Those who sow in tears shall reap in joy." (Psalm 126:5).* Not sure about you, but I like the 'reap in joy' part the best. We hear about joy a lot but are we joyful? Does it take work to be happy? We give no thought about being upset: we just are. But joy, peace, and gratitude for our Savior: those behaviors need to be learned. *"Teach me Your way, O Lord; I will walk in Your truth; unite my heart to fear Your name. I will praise You, O Lord my God, with all my heart, and I will glorify Your name forevermore. For great is Your mercy toward me, and You have delivered my soul from the depths of Sheol." (Psalm 86:11-13).*

Great is God's mercy and yet He is our teacher. When you were in school did you have a favorite teacher? Did you look forward to spending time in his/her class? Was there ever a time when your teacher extended mercy towards you? God is our ultimate teacher. Unlike the world's class where there is a possibility of failure, there is no failure in God's class. We don't fail, we just go around and around the mountain. There is no time frame as to when we have to complete the course. God's class is a lifelong journey.

God's class may not be based on grades but learning does have advantages. We can stop going around the mountain and enjoy some new scenery. We begin to develop into the person God created us to be. Peace, joy, gratitude all become our natural state of being. There is a condition to God's classroom: you must want to be there.

All we have to do is ask. We learn from *James 1:5, "If any of you lacks wisdom, let him ask of God, who gives to all liberally and without reproach, and it will be given to him."* When you want to see if something works: try it. Thank God for His goodness and ask Him to help you excel in His class.

Help Me Be a Servant *(2007)*

I'm so thankful that I'm here

It's the Lord, I feel Him near

I'm so thankful when I hear

God speaking softly in my ear

Tell me Lord what I should do

To be of service unto you

All I want is for your will

Use me Lord; your will fulfill

Ask and you shall receive. Well I asked. On break at work I was sitting in my car and reading the verse from my pocket, *"Finally, all of you be of one mind, having compassion for one another; love as brothers, be tenderhearted, be courteous..." (1Peter 3:8).* While I was meditating on the verse and watching a bird build its nest I said to God, "Lord, I try to encourage people and tell them about Your love. What do You want me to learn from this scripture?" And it just kind of hit me yes, I do pray with and for people, yes, I try to encourage them *but* who am I missing?

We seem to have a specific set of people in our lives and a routine in the way we interact with them. How often do we slip out of our comfort zone and welcome a stranger? I'm sure there are some of you who do but others maybe need a little encouragement in this area. Sometimes all we have to do is look around; God will put people in our path. Don't be surprised if you are working on this area of your faith walk, and when you ask God to use you it might be for a stranger that you may never even meet. God may prompt you to simply pray for someone. I know that sounds strange, but that is exactly what happened.

A Prayer for a Stranger (2011)

She was sitting in her car
Newspaper in her hand
Staring at help wanted ads
Thoughts lost; in no man's land.

The tears they start to fall
As she makes another call
Again came the reply,
"I'm sorry, we've already hired.
Thank you for calling, good bye."

I saw her spirit begin to fade
I can't take this, her expression seemed to say
It was then God touched my heart
So I began to pray

"God, I don't know her story
But you let me notice her
So Father, to you be the glory
As your love lets her know you're near."

I watched her drive away,
Then I stopped again to say:
"God, thank You for a chance to pray
For a stranger on this glorious July day."

Not all acts of faith are to be noticed, some are for God alone. Be faithful in small things because people are watching.

Are you aware that you continually lead by example? We are the representatives of Christ. *"By this all will know that you are My disciples, if you have love for one another." (John 13:35).* Love for one another means at home, work and play not only in the church parking lot. Since others are watching, what do you say... we go ahead and talk to them?

Talk to them? What, you want me to talk to people? Yes, just like you have done probably most of your life. Help somebody with a need and when they ask you why, share your faith. There is a lot of work to be done for the kingdom. *"Behold, I say to you, lift up your eyes and look at the fields, for they are already white for harvest! And he who reaps receives wages, and gathers fruit for eternal life, that both he who sows and he who reaps may rejoice together. For in this the saying is true: 'One sows and another reaps.' I sent you to reap that for which you have not labored; others have labored, and you have entered into their labors." (John 4:35-38).*

The Seed (2010)

The seed was planted in her heart by a stranger who passed by
Now she lay there in the dark; the words caused her to cry

"God...loves...you..."rang in her ears; "He sent Jesus to die"
Her mind was spinning full of fear..., as she wondered... was it a lie?

If you're real then show me God was all that she could ask
The seed was **planted** in the sod of a heart... broken by the past

While sitting on the subway, facing yet another day
She noticed a man praying and asked why... would he pray

With joyous smile and twinkling eyes, she finally heard him speak
I couldn't walk a mile, Miss, without God... I'm way too weak

Again her heart was churning, like the turning of the tide
"What if God is really... real?" was the thought she could not hide

The planted seed was **watered**, from the fountain of God's love
As God reached down and touched her heart from the heavens high above

She noticed a boy playing on the rocks beside the creek
She walked a little closer, just to take a peek

The rock the boy handed her stopped her in her tracks
She looked and found within the rock... a cross was looking back

She wondered aloud, about the cross... and what it all could mean
The boy said its simple Mama..., Jesus died... for you and me

Now... the child could lead her... to the Savior, oh so true
For now her heart was ready, and **the boy knew what to do**

If you …say yes to Jesus and give Him all your heart
He will live inside you and from you… He'll never part

The **seed** became a soul…who will live in eternity
Planted, watered, and **harvested**; by children of the King!

Planted, watered, harvested sounds like a lot of work if you had to do it alone but we are not alone. We do it together. God places people at the right place and the right time. I heard Pastor Joel Osteen in his sermon, "It's Your Due Season," mention a divine connection. You might be someone's divine connection and all you have to do is talk? Here is a question to ponder: Do you think God made us such fluent talkers, not speakers, just plain conversationalists so we had no excuse not to share our faith? Husbands and wives alike could argue...with love of course... if you claim you don't talk.

I hope you are encouraged to start sharing Jesus stories with your friends. You know God will give you the words; trust Him, He never fails. Do you realize there are as many different ways to share your faith as there are stars that you can see on a clear night?

I love the stars. Each one is different. *"There is one glory of the sun, another glory of the moon, and another glory of the stars; for one star differs from another star in glory." (1Corinthians 15:41).* We can't create the stars they are a gift from God, the creator of heaven and earth. I hope your sky is clear tonight so you can enjoy the stars.

Reassurance *(2007)*

I could never count them
The stars up in the sky
God placed them there to show me
He is my guiding light

At night when I lie down to sleep
The pillow beneath my head
I look out of my window
And wonder what's ahead

I see the stars up in the sky
And know that God is near
Then I sleep so peacefully
With no worry and no fear

I thank God He takes the time
To show me that He cares
And the stars they do remind me
He is always there

On a day when you need a lift look up at the clouds floating by, but at night enjoy the stars. Both are free gifts from our Father. If you are a parent you understand how it feels giving your children presents. I think God feels the same way about His children.

Parents and Children

A tangled web of love

"To the Lord our God belong mercy and forgiveness..."
(Daniel 9:9)

I believe children have a special place in God's heart. God is the creator and provider for all. We know how He takes care of us but have you ever thought about what happens to the wildlife families? The Bible tells us that God has a plan for everything: *"Therefore I say to you, do not worry about your life, what you will eat or what you will drink...Look at the birds of the air, for they neither sow nor reap nor gather into barns; yet your heavenly Father feeds them. Are you not of more value than they... For your heavenly Father knows that you need all these things."* (Matthew 6:25-26,32).

Then Jesus explained how and where the birds reside. *"... a mustard seed, which a man took and sowed in his field,...and becomes a tree, so that the birds of the air come and nest in its branches."* (Matthew 13:31-32). Whether it is food or housing God has all of us covered.

I was able to witness God's love expressed through a mother bird. It was mesmerizing to watch. I kept thinking what a wonderful example she was setting. She was so full of love for her babies you could watch her compassion and patience come to life.

Leaving the Nest (2007)

I saw the momma bird take flight, with babies right behind
She only flew a little way, their wings were yet too fine

She waited on the fence to see, if they would come along
Three were perched upon the ledge, the fourth was not so strong

His body lifted in the air, and then he fell back down
I watched this happen several times, till the others he had found

Now four were perched upon the ledge, and Momma flew back around
To see that all the babies, had safely lifted from the ground

She flew back to the fence, making sure they all could see
Then sang a song so sweetly saying,
"It's safe to come to me"

One by one they followed her, so tentative and so shy
And when they all had reached her, she turned again to fly

From fence, to chair, and across the porch, they followed close behind
Then they rested for a while, warmed in the bright sunshine

She sang to them so softly they listened, to her voice so kind
When she finished they sang to her, tiny voices so refined

Then Momma flew into the tree that grows beside the porch
The babies followed close behind, guided by love and not by force

All summer they sang so sweetly, from the branches of the tree
And I thank God for sharing, His special treat with me

Children are a precious gift from God. When I was 17 I was told I would never have a child. Fast forward almost a decade and voila I am going to be a mommy.

The first three months all the doctors wanted to discuss was abortion. No, God created this child and He would see me through. I kept the faith. That became harder as I continued to lose weight. I kept the faith. Two days prior to a natural birth the doctors decided the baby would be underweight and would need to be flown to a children's hospital. I kept the faith. Full term due date arrived, I kept the faith; when the doctor told the nurse to cancel the chopper, I thanked God for faith. Jason is now a husband, a father, and a veteran.

We want to do things for our children. The most important thing we can do is found in *Deuteronomy 11:18-19 "...lay up these words of mine in your heart and in your soul...You shall teach them to your children, speaking of them when you sit in your house, when you walk by the way, when you lie down, and when you rise up."* We lead by example, important to remember as we teach our children about Jesus and His love.

A Mother's Love (1980)

It took a while for me to see
Just what a Mother's love could be
A while to understand and know
The way in which the love would grow

At first it seemed to me I knew
All the things a mother must do
Then each day it seemed to me
I knew very little for a mother-to-be

In the beginning it was a dream not real
Then suddenly you see the baby you feel
You know in your heart, mind, body and soul
That this is a dream, a mother's true goal

To take this moment you feel each day
And hold in your arms, in your own special way
This bundle of joy, love and yes, tension too
And do all the things a mother can do

You realize it's not easy to know from the start
How to express all the feelings you hide in your heart
But a baby you see comes from two full of love
So share all with each other and the one up above.

Babies are so full of love and awareness, they learn so quickly and they notice everything. Mistakes will be made; I made more than the stars you could count. Know that God does not leave when you become a parent. I think He may be even closer if that is possible. Like Jesus, offer unconditional love. Jason's dad, Chuck, was the epitome of unconditional love. He was the first to sit down on the floor and play. Before we relocated he was attending a discipleship class and he knew: *"All your children shall be taught by the Lord, and great shall be the peace of your children." (Isaiah 54:13).* I remember the first time we were hanging out in the living room and Chuck opened the Bible and started telling Jason the story of Noah; Jason loved water and toys that floated, so an ark, animals, and a flood were the perfect place to start.

Then there was the day that Jason once again loaded his indoor dump truck up with dirt from a large potted plant. He had just learned how it all worked together. Before he talked to Jason, Chuck told me I have to do this and showed me, *"Train up a child in the way he should go, and when he is old he will not depart from it."(Proverbs 22:6).* Jason learned the word honor; he could hardly say it but he knew what it meant.

When Jason was about six months old, after enjoying a family day and watching both of them sleeping, Jason across Chuck's chest, the still small voice gave me the following...

Understanding Father (1981)

If fathers could show, their feelings so true,
There'd be hardness and laughter, and lots of love for you.

You're the offspring he hoped for, a part of his own,
The one who will carry his name, when he's gone.

The dreams that he had, which never panned out,
Might be what he hopes for you, so... just look out.

Although he might be, gruff in his way,
He only wants the best for you, day after day.

As he watches you grow, from boy into man,
You may do a lot of things, he doesn't understand.

And trouble if ever, must come on your way,
He'll be there behind you, and that's where he'll stay.

To be there and help you, with all of his might,
From your knees if you fall, back to full height.

So if he seems mean and you don't understand,
Remember he traveled from boyhood to man.

And many the times, he says, "No" to your face,
May just be why... you're thankful, later on in life's race.

Just think of his hardness, laughter and love,
As divine guidance from the Father above.

If ever you lie there, hating him; all through the night,
Today you might see, you turned out alright

Don't wait to thank him, and tell him with love,
You're glad he's your Father, the man that you love

Being loved by your children is a blessing. My Mom is a seasoned Christian who walks in complete unquestioning faith. When it comes to living for the Lord she lives by example. We lived in Chicago in the 60's and our church was having a Sunday school competition to see who could bring the most visitors. Well my brother Mike and I knew that asking a couple of close friends was not going to cut it. We tried, but alas Mom meant kingdom work. We won the contest but that is not the part that sticks with me.

There was a family of four or five who we invited. Back in those days you had church clothes. This family had nothing; I was young and I am not even certain now that they were not living in a car. Every Saturday night Mom brought the whole family over. Clothes were washed and ironed, baths were taken, hair was set and they stayed till after church on Sunday. Please understand we lived in a two-bedroom one-bath apartment. Mom taught us by example: *"And whoever gives one of these little ones only a cup of cold water in the name of a disciple, assuredly, I say to you, he shall by no means lose his reward."* (Matthew 10:42).

My Mom (1981)

What is a Mother? Oh, what can I say?
All the words have been used, to describe all their ways.

Their special look of love, that comes to the eyes,
When out of paper and glue, you make a surprise.

Mothers are there, when you skin your knees,
With band aids and kisses, and cookies if you please.

Then when you grow older, ready to date,
Mothers are waiting, if you come in late.

Worry and love, Smiles and yes, tears,
This is what carries, A "Mom" through,
the years.

So if you don't think, your "Mom" really cares,
Just remember the years that *Mom* was always there.

Parents are loved and loving; what a beautiful gift from above. It is fun to watch new parents with their infant, they just beam with joy. I also like to watch newborn animals. It does not really matter what kind. The ugliest baby animal alive looks adorable to me. Ok I admit I have an empty snuggly spot for babies of all kinds. We know they are precious: God created them.

I was near Lake Tahoe in the 70's; we had been riding snowmobiles and stopped by the side of a small frozen pond. It was slightly warm, the sun was shining, the snow was glistening and I spotted a fawn with its mom. The baby wanted to come out on the pond but Mom was not so sure. Eventually she gave in and they inched their way across the pond about to the center.

That is when my imagination kicked in and I started thinking about the scripture, *"The wolf also shall dwell with the lamb…and a little child shall lead them. The cow and the bear shall graze; their young ones shall lie down together…" (Isaiah 11:6-7).* This was the first time I heard the still small voice. I was young and just starting to recognize that God was whispering to me.

Playing in the Snow (1975)

Snowflakes falling from the sky
Bring a twinkle to your eyes
Paint the world a silent white
Fall so peaceful in the night

Children bundled from the cold
Built a snowman I am told
As you watch from window near
Could it be you see a deer?

Brought her little fawn to play
On this peaceful snowy day
The children stop as she comes near
Showing the babe there's nothing to fear

Parents stand on either side
Smiling faces show their pride
As fawn and children both alike
Frolic in the snowy white

Thoughts About the Future

What plans have you made?

"For 'whoever calls on the name of the LORD shall be saved.'" (Romans 10:13)

God our Father sets the example for how things should be in our families. Many families have unique situations; ours was one of those families.

For years, actually decades, I searched for my siblings. I guess you could say it was a desperately lonely obsession. During that time I spent many hours crying out to God. I had a Bible my mom had given me, which I still have today. I searched it high and low for a promise God would reunite my family. One of the scriptures I held onto was, *"Therefore do not cast away your confidence, which has great reward. For you have need of endurance, so that after you have done the will of God, you may receive the promise: 'For yet a little while, and He who is coming will come and will not tarry. Now the just shall live by faith...'" (Hebrews 10:35-38).*

I am ecstatic to share that after almost 25 years I found my brother, Mike, and sister, Michelle. It was less than a year later I found Linda; we had been separated for over 30 years. I was convinced we would not be reunited until we reached heaven. To my joy God had a different plan. It is never too late. God will answer in His timing.

Going Home *(1991)*

God's my shoulder, God's my rock
My life He set by His own clock
The roads I go He did not choose
But His love for me I will not lose

My road He planned is narrow and straight
I see Him standing just past the gate
With arms outstretched and opened wide
When finally home I'll be by His side

Then my family He'll give to me
Making my heart full and free
For now I cling to His hand tight
I know the gate is just out of sight

Each day I live brings me closer to home
Where finally in peace and happiness I'll roam.

Going home to heaven...it sounds so rapturous. We miss those who have passed away and we all share heartache but sometimes the living are left with regrets.
God has given us ways to help us eliminate the need for a second chance. *"...put on tender mercies, kindness, humility, meekness, longsuffering; bearing with one another, and forgiving one another, if anyone has a complaint against another; even as Christ forgave you, so you also must do. But above all these things put on love, which is the bond of perfection. And let the peace of God rule in your hearts... and be thankful." (Colossians 3:12-15).*

In 2014 I found myself walking down memory lane. Jason's father Chuck passed away. How many of you know divorce can be a slippery slope? Even though we had been divorced for almost 30 years and some of it a rocky road, you still wonder: do I have any regrets? If he had passed a few years earlier the answer would have been yes. But he called me several times after Jon's passing and eventually all that needed to be said was. We had arrived at a peaceful resolution. Neither of us was getting younger; we needed to have a clean slate. I thank God we fought to work it out.

No Second Chances Needed (2014)

<u>Regrets:</u>
I wish I would have_____
I wonder if I could have_____
I know I really should have_____

<u>Reasons:</u>
Procrastination, questioning, guilt

<u>Results:</u>
I'm spinning like a weather vane on a very windy day

<u>Reverse:</u>
I am glad I did_____
My actions made the difference_____
End results couldn't have been better_____

<u>Reasons:</u>
Taking action, decision implemented, accomplishment

<u>Results:</u>
I'm sitting on a swing on a warm summer day enjoying the cool breeze

Opportunities taken have no need for second chances.

We all leave this world the same way. Where we spend eternity depends on the decisions we make. *"...for the Son of Man has come to seek and to save that which was lost."* (Luke 19:10). God sent His only son for our redemption. What more could God offer to show how sincerely He cares about us? I believe in death there are only two places: heaven or hell. God leaves the choice up to us. He wants us to choose eternity with Him but He gave us free will. If we want to spend eternity in heaven then remember what we are taught: *"Jesus said to him, 'I am the way, the truth, and the life. No one comes to the Father except through Me.'"* (John 14:6).

I was reading Pastor Kerry Shook's book, "Be the Message," he is talking about the first step. He writes: "Truth is, I don't need to have my life together, and I'm not 'just one person.' God's on my side. And maybe you've noticed: He's a difference maker." If you want a change in your life, a friend who is closer than a brother, a savior then I invite you to do as I did when I wrote the following poem. It is the only one in this book not from the still small voice; it was and is from my heart.

Commitment (1970)

Lord I know that I come to you in sorrow
Lord I know that I come to you in shame
Only by your help I will make it through tomorrow
But mistakes I make will never be the same

Today I asked for my sins to be forgiven
And I know they're buried in the deepest sea
A new life for you now I've started living
Since you opened up your heart and pardoned me

I am a babe in this new life that I am living
For I know through your word that you'll feed me
I read the Bible that helps keep me from sinning
And with my life now I will walk close to thee

Please Lord help me if I start to fall and stumble
For this way I have chosen is new to me
Help me to forget myself and remain humble
This dear Lord is my desire and my plea

I hope you enjoyed our time together. May the poems encourage you along your journey of growth. I am asking God to guide, protect, and comfort you always. Before we part I have a question for you.

What would YOU say is God's greatest gift?

Some would say Christmas. Jesus agreed to be born into the world. He lived among mankind for 33 years as our life's example. Christmas is God giving us a savior.

Others would say Easter. At the age of 33 Jesus died for our sins. Easter the holiday when even secular businesses will close. Easter service is one of the highest spikes in church attendance regardless of denomination. Easter is Jesus enduring our salvation.

I believe that everyone should consider that the greatest gift from God to humanity is Mercy.

Christmas is covered by Mercy. For without sin there would have been no need for a savior to be born. Christmas: Jesus entering the world as a newborn.

Easter is covered by Mercy. Very few if any humans have ever been as vexed in spirit as to sweat drops of blood. Not Jesus' will but God's will be done. God's will is that humans have a way of redemption. What would it cost? What could come close to paying the price of mankind's sin? Only one held such value: God's only son, Jesus. So for God's price to be met, our salvation was purchased by

Jesus' enduring death on the cross AND His resurrection from the tomb.

Why would God desire and Jesus agree to fulfill such a plan? MERCY.

Mercy brought me my savior, Jesus. Mercy gave me the gift of redemption through Jesus' resurrection. Mercy covers me every moment of my life. For me God's greatest gift is MERCY.

You can experience salvation and share God's gift of mercy by asking Jesus to be your savior. I would feel privileged to lead you in the following prayer:

"Dear Lord Jesus, come into my heart. I ask you to be my Lord and Savior. I believe you died on the cross for ALL mankind. I believe you rose again on the third day and now reside in heaven. Please forgive me of my sins. I come to you in childlike faith. Help me Lord to grow in your ways. I want to live for you. You said you will not leave me nor forsake me. I take You at Your word. In Jesus holy name I pray. Amen."

Date I became a child of the King:

_____

If you have a Bible please start to read it. The book of John is a good place to start. If you are not familiar with the Bible, the Living version of the Bible is very easy to understand. If you would like a more in-depth study try an Amplified Bible. Find a Bible-believing, spirit-filled church; they can help you grow.

May life treat you and yours well
May your days be filled with sunshine and happiness
May your rainy days always end with a double rainbow
May God continue to watch over you

www.ingramcontent.com/pod-product-compliance
Lightning Source LLC
Chambersburg PA
CBHW071310060426
42444CB00034B/1766